EL DORADO

Optimise your options trading

Written by Owen O'Malley, CEO of TICN Ltd., and James Garza, CTO of TICN Ltd.

Editing, cover design and illustrations by Ana Rodríguez, CEO of TICN Spain

www.ticn.com

Investment Club Network are not in any way liable for your activities or purchases resulting from information obtained at this Money Talk or in the handout.

There is risk of loss in all trading and investing. Past performance is not necessarily a guide to future performance and all investment can go down as well as up. You should read the Chicago Board of Options Exchange booklet, entitled *Characteristics and risks of standardized options* before trading options. You should understand the risks in option trading including the fact that any time an option is sold, there is unlimited risk of loss, and when an option is purchased, the entire premium is at risk. In addition, any time an option is purchased or sold, transaction costs, including brokerage and exchange fees are at risk. No representation is made regarding the success of our recommendations or that any account is likely to achieve profits or losses similar to those shown, or in any amount. Any account may experience different results depending on the timing of trades and account size. Trading is risky, and many traders lose money. Before trading, one should be aware that with the potential for profits, there is also potential for losses which may be large. All opinions are subject to change without notice.

Because of the dynamic nature of the Internet, any Web addresses or links contained in this book may have changed since publication and may no longer be valid. The views expressed in this work are solely those of the author and do not

Acknowledgments

We would like to take this opportunity to thank all the members of TICN that have chosen to join us. Our desire is to inspire you all to become Financially Free.

A special word of thanks to our TICN leaders, tutors and the TICN Support Team. Without you, we could not do what we do. Thank you all so much.

TABLE OF CONTENTS

Chapter   **Page**

Chapter 1

Introduction

To understand and follow the contents of this book, it would be recommended to read our first book: *So… you want to be Financially Free?* at http://www.tinyurl.com/previewticnbook.

This book also assumes that you are familiar with the chart indicators to know when to buy low and sell high. In summary, you should at this stage know how to recognise when the chart is at the bottom of the 3rd roll in a downward trend with:

1) the stochastic lines < 20 with the "V" for victory

2) the RSI line < 30 with the "V" for victory

3) hidden strength after maximum negative length in the MACD bars

to signify the best time to buy stock, sell puts and buy calls.

Likewise, you know when to recognise that the chart is at the top of the 3rd roll of an upward trend with:

4) the stochastic lines > 80 with the upside down "V"

5) the RSI line > 70 with the upside down "V" for victory

6) hidden weakness after maximum positive length in the MACD bars

to signify the best time to sell stock, sell calls and buy puts.

If you already have experience of selling calls and selling puts, this book will help you increase your performance by one or two percent extra per month. This extra performance is provided that you read, learn and apply the strategies taught in this *El Dorado* book.

This book also assumes that you are familiar with the Mytrack Software and, more importantly, the Option Display to be able to get all the information referred to in the following chapters.

Introduction to Options

In our basic **MMCP Making Money** with **Careful Planning** Seminar, you learn that options have two parts to their valuation:

1) Real Value (or Intrinsic Value)

2) Time Value

In the example as below, we show you how to identify the difference between the time value and real value of an option:

Price of a $10 call option.......................................: $0.81
Market price of share..: $10.46
Strike price of the option to buy the share........: $10
Real value of the option ....:
    market price minus strike price
Therefore, <u>real value</u> of the option.....................:
    $10.46 - $10 ....= $<u>0.46</u>

This means that if the $10 option was to be used to buy the shares at the agreed strike price of $10 and the shares were immediately sold back to the market at the market price of $10.46, the trade would yield a profit of $10.46 minus the $10, which is $0.46. This is, therefore, the underline real value of the option.

Now, if the total price of option is $0.81 and we have established the real value is $0.46, the time value is the difference between both values as follows:

Time Value = Option Price minus Real Value
Time Value = $0.81 - $0.46 = $0.35

The time value of an option can be compared to that of an ice cube: let us imagine we have an ice cube sitting on top of the open palm of our hand and we are stading 30 steps away from a bonfire. As we walk to the bonfire, the ice melts down. 30 steps represent 30 days to go to expiration date.

For every step you take towards the fire, the more the ice cube is melting in your hand as it is subjected to the intense heat from the large fire. Once you get to the fire, which represents the time of the closing bell of the option market on the expiration date, and throw the ice cube into the fire, it ceases to exist just like an option ceases to exist after the expiration date.

Option Price = Real Value + Time Value

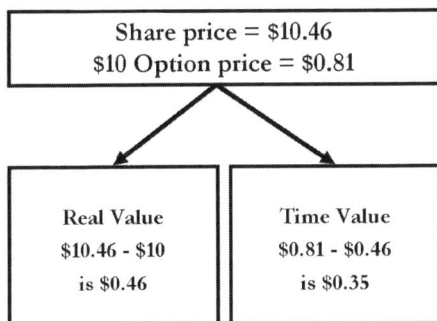

```
┌─────────────────────────────────────────┐
│           Share price = $10.46           │
│        $10 Option price = $0.81          │
└─────────────────────────────────────────┘
```

```
┌──────────────────┐  ┌──────────────────┐
│    Real Value    │  │    Time Value    │
│   $10.46 - $10   │  │  $0.81 - $0.46   │
│    is $0.46      │  │    is $0.35      │
└──────────────────┘  └──────────────────┘
```

We are now in a position to take your understanding of options to the next level and explain to you that Time Value is further divided into:

1) Historical Volatility and

2) Implied Volatility

Historical Volatility is a measure of how much the share price has moved or fluctuated from the annual high price to the annual low price in the past 52 weeks. This value can be found on the top right hand side of the Option Display in your Mytrack Trading Software program. (To find your option display, right click on the ticker symbol of a company and then left click on Option Display).

Last Price	Change	High	Low	DivAmt	DivDate	AnnHI	AnnLOW	EPS	Volatility
7.15	--			0.00	12/30/99	16.59	5.44	0.00	54

If, for example, the Volatility figure displays as 54, this means that the share price has moved plus 54% and minus 54% from the average price over the previous 52 weeks. Using this annual figure of 54 and dividing by 12 months (54/12 = 4.5), it would be safe to assume that it would be perfectly normal for the share price to fluctuate at least ±4.5% in the next month.

Time Value = Implied + Historical Volatility

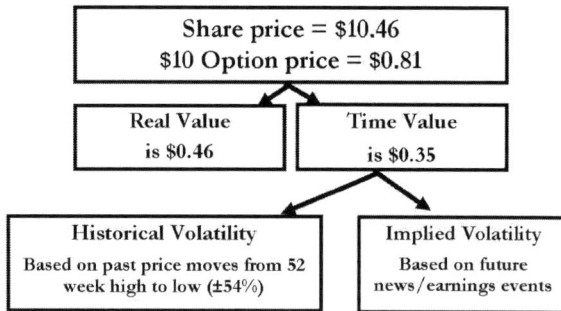

Share price = $10.46
$10 Option price = $0.81

Real Value
is $0.46

Time Value
is $0.35

Historical Volatility
Based on past price moves from 52 week high to low (±54%)

Implied Volatility
Based on future news/earnings events

Implied Volatility is a reflection of any significant impending news that is about to happen in the next month. An example of a very significant news event would be the date of the next company quarterly sales and profit (known as Earnings Report). This explains why, in the period of three to four weeks before an earnings report, the option prices can double or even in some cases triple in value. Later on this book, we will be explaining to you and giving you examples of how you can profit from these extraordinary high option prices.

Once the news event has happened, option prices will immediately return to normal prices. For example, the normal monthly % available during normal times with no significant news is 2 – 3% per 30 day period of time (for shares that trade between $5 and $25 and have options that trade in volumes of 1,000 or more). However, in the three to four week time period before the news event, these prices can become as high as 4% to 9% per 30 day period of time.

Once you have found the Option Display in Mytrack, you can find the Call Vega (c_vega) and Call Implied Volatility (c_iv) by right clicking on one of the headings and left clicking on the dropdown menu item.

Preferences More								Option Display	
BBRY	Last Price 7.15	Change —	High	Low	DivAmt 0.00	DivDate 12/30/99	AnnHI 16.59	AnnLOW 5.44	EPS 0.00
%out 50	⦿ Composite	○ All							

04/25/14	05/02/14	05/09/14	May/2014	05/23/14	05/30/14	Jun/2
c_name	c_ask	c_bid	c_int	c_tmval	c_iv	c_vega	dexp
BBRY May14 4 C	3.35	3.00	3.15	-.15	100	.000	29
BBRY May14 5 C	2.35	2.05	2.15	-.10	87	.000	29
BBRY May14 6 C	1.23	1.21	1.15	.06	55	.004	29
BBRY May14 7 C	.48	.47	.15	.32	50	.008	29
BBRY May14 8 C	.16	.15		.15	54	.007	29
BBRY May14 9 C	.05	.04		.04	57	.003	29
BBRY May14 10 C	.03	.02		.02	65	.001	29

Time Value = Implied + Historical Volatility

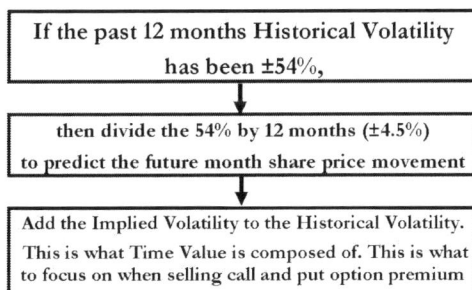

If the past 12 months Historical Volatility has been ±54%,

then divide the 54% by 12 months (±4.5%) to predict the future month share price movement

Add the Implied Volatility to the Historical Volatility. This is what Time Value is composed of. This is what to focus on when selling call and put option premium

Thus, in summary, to calculate the time value of an option, the market makers use a combination of past volatility and future (implied) volatility to help price options. One can use this understanding and new information to make much higher returns from selling call and put options in the future.

In fact, we have seen many of our students and club members and clubs significantly increase their percentage monthly return after attending our one day **El Dorado Options** course.

Introduction to Option Greeks

Some Greek letters can be used to predict how option prices will behave in the future. In this chapter, we will focus in the following ones:

1) Delta

2) Theta

3) Vega

4) Rho

Delta

Delta is a very handy tool to predict the price of an option in the future.

Delta measures the relationship between the share price movement and the option price movement. In this regard, one can find out if the share price rises by $1 by how much will the option price increase by.

In the Option Display, the Delta is known as the Hedge Ratio (Hedge = h and Ratio = R) and so is displayed as c_hr or p_hr in the Option Display (c = call and p = put options)

Option Greeks - Delta

<u>Delta</u> is used to help predict by how much an option price will increase or decrease relative to the increase or decrease of the underlying share price that the option is derived from

Delta is known as the <u>Hedge Ratio (hr)</u>
Delta is labelled in the Option Display
as c_hr for Call Delta and p_hr for Put Delta

In the example as below:

Share price ....: $10.46
Call option price ....: $1.48
Delta of the call option....................................: 0.58

If share price rises by $1,
the Option will rise by $0.58, and the
Option price will increase from $1.48
to $1.48 + $0.58 = $2.06.

How to use Delta to predict option prices

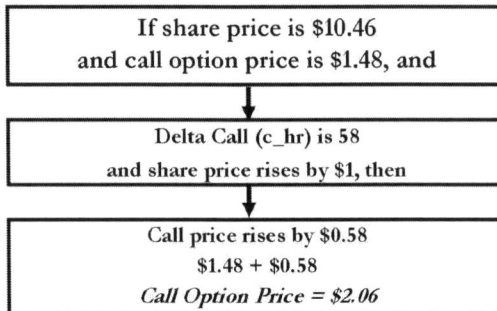

If share price is $10.46 and call option price is $1.48, and

Delta Call (c_hr) is 58 and share price rises by $1, then

Call price rises by $0.58 $1.48 + $0.58 *Call Option Price = $2.06*

In the second example as below:

Share price ....: $10.46
Call option ....: $1.48
Delta of the call option..................................: 0.58

If share price rises by $0.40,
the Option will rise by $0.58 x $0.40 = $0.23 and the
Option price will increase from $1.48
to $1.48 + $0.23 = $1.71

How to use Delta to predict option prices

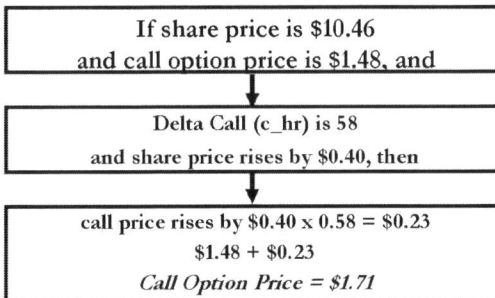

If share price is $10.46 **and call option price is $1.48, and**

Delta Call (c_hr) is 58 **and share price rises by $0.40, then**

call price rises by $0.40 x 0.58 = $0.23 $1.48 + $0.23 *Call Option Price = $1.71*

In the third example as below:

Share price ....: $10.46
Put option price ....: $0.66
Delta of the put option..................................: -0.42

If share price falls by $0.40, the
Option will rise by $0.40 x 0.42 = $0.17, and the
Put Option price will increase from $0.66
to $0.66 + $0.17 = $0.83

How to use Delta to predict option prices

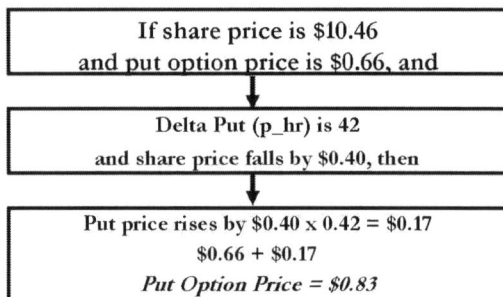

If share price is $10.46 and put option price is $0.66, and

↓

Delta Put (p_hr) is 42 and share price falls by $0.40, then

↓

Put price rises by $0.40 x 0.42 = $0.17 $0.66 + $0.17 *Put Option Price = $0.83*

Delta Sweet Spot

One would think that the relationship between the rise of the share price and the increase in the option delta should be in a straight line relationship. However, there is not a straight line relationship between the share price rise and the option delta.

If you study the graph as below, you will notice that between an option delta values from 0 to 70 there is a delayed reaction of the delta to the rise in share price. Once the delta value gets to 70, there is a more than normal rise in the value of the option delta as the option now has to catch up with and compensate for the previous delayed reaction. This causes an above average rate of increase in the value of the option deltas.

The Option Sweet Spot is between a delta of 70 and 90 as this is where you will get the fastest response time to a slight increase in the share price.

So one of the Rules to buying options is to make sure that you are purchasing the option when the delta is already at or as close as is possible to 70. Once the delta value gets to 90, the increase in value will return to a normal straight line relationship as there is no longer a need for an above average rate of increase in the value of the option.

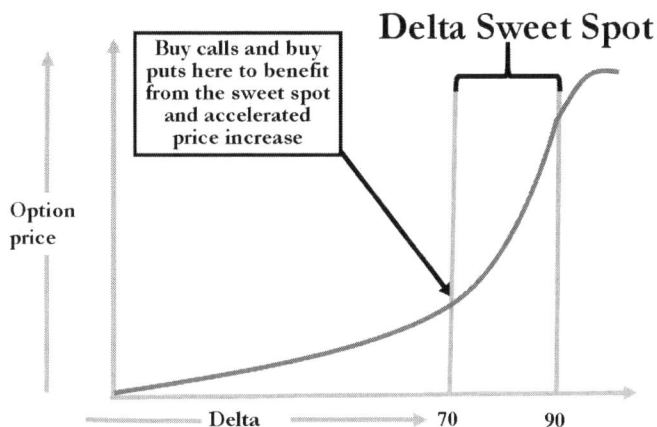

In summary, the delta is a handy tool to help predict the option price movement in the future. Sometimes, you can observe a delayed reaction of the option price increase to share price increase in that the share price will rise and then, 20 to 30 minutes later, the option price will move.

Knowing this, you have to learn to be patient in that if you have an order in place GTC (Good Til Cancelled) to sell an option for a higher price than it currently is, you may have to wait 20 to 30 minutes for the order to be filled.

However, when the share price falls, option prices react immediately and will fall at the same rate with no delayed reaction.

Theta

Theta is used to measure the time value of option and how much this time value will erode per day between now and the number of days to the option expiration day.

Let us visualise an option as an ice cube that will melt every day, therefore, getting smaller every day until the day after the option expiration day, when it will cease to exist.

In this scenario, theta measures by how much the option ice cube will melt per day. Options that are ATM or At The Money (meaning the share price in the market and the strike price of the option are the same value) will have the highest Theta values.

Option Greeks - Theta

Theta is used to measure time decay of an option

Theta is expressed in how many cents per day
that an option will lose its time value

It applies to both call options and put options

Theta is labelled in the Option Display
as c_theta for Call Theta and p_theta for Put Theta
The At The Money (ATM) options have the highest Theta

In example 1 as below:

Days to expiration ....: 30
Call option price ....: $1.00
Theta..: 0.05

On the next day, 29 days to expiration ....: - 1 day
Time value of the option, decreased by ......: $0.05
$1.00 - $0.05 = $0.95

Therefore, by waiting an extra day to sell an option in this example, you would incur a lost opportunity to collect an income of $0.05 per share for the month: the more days you delay selling an option, the more opportunity you lose to make money.

Remember: the goal is to sell as much time value as possible every month. We call the time value of an option the 'free money' that is there to be collected every month.

How to use Theta to predict option prices

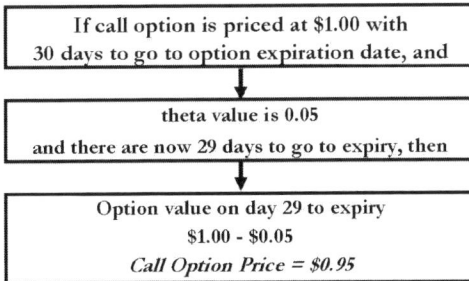

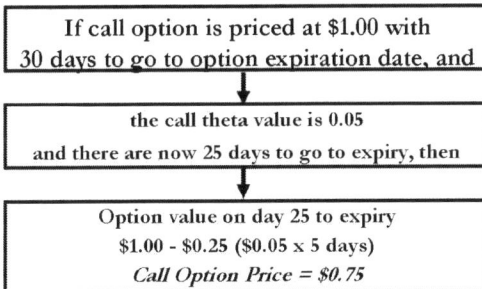

If call option is priced at $1.00 with 30 days to go to option expiration date, and

↓

theta value is 0.05 and there are now 29 days to go to expiry, then

↓

Option value on day 29 to expiry $1.00 - $0.05 *Call Option Price = $0.95*

In example 2 as below:

Days to expiration ....: 30
Call option price ....: $1.00
Theta..: 0.05

On the next day, 25 days to expiration ....: - 5 days
Time value of the option, decreased by ......:
    $0.05x5days=$0.25
$1.00 - $0.25 = $0.75

How to use Theta to predict option prices

If call option is priced at $1.00 with 30 days to go to option expiration date, and

↓

the call theta value is 0.05 and there are now 25 days to go to expiry, then

↓

Option value on day 25 to expiry $1.00 - $0.25 ($0.05 x 5 days) *Call Option Price = $0.75*

Examine the graph of theta or time value of an option over a 90 day time period of time.

Notice that the option time value will hold most of its value in the first 45 days.

Then, you will notice that the time value will lose most of its time value in the last 45 days.

When you are buying options, you will want to buy with 60 to 90 days to go to expiration.

This increases your chances of success in a trade if you are buying options, since the time value will be stable while you are waiting for your anticipated movement in the share price to happen.

When you are selling options, you will want to sell with 45 days to 30 days to go to expiration.

You would like to sell the call option when it has maximum time value and then observe the option time value reduce in your favour over time.

Theta - Option Time decay curve

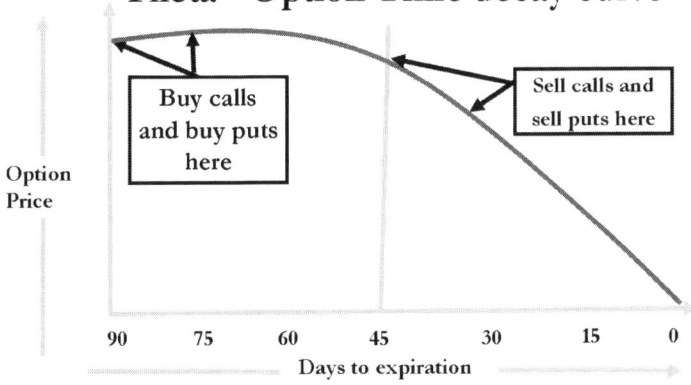

Option Price

Buy calls and buy puts here

Sell calls and sell puts here

90   75   60   45   30   15   0

Days to expiration

Most of the time value can be collected with 45 days to 30 days to expiration, as illustrated above.

Vega

Vega measures the rate of change in the implied volatility of an option time value.

The goal when selling options is to sell as much time value and volatility as possible.

The majority of the time value and volatility are to be found close to the ATM options.

The objective when buying options is to avoid buying time value and volatility.

The least amount of time value and volatility is to be found either side of the ATM options.

By buying ITM options, you capture the higher delta values.

Vega - Time Value Volatility

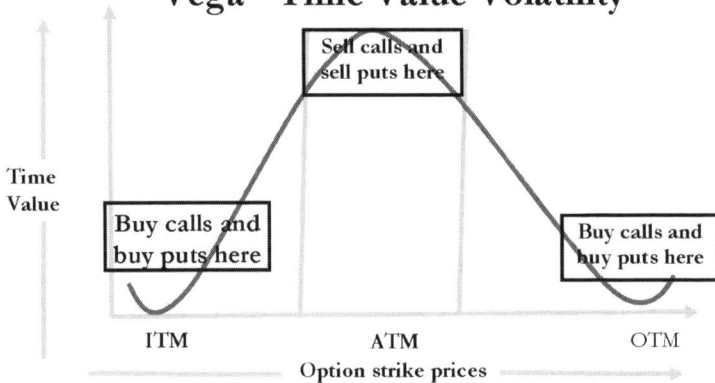

Future news events and impending earnings reports have the greatest impact on the rate of change of the implied volatility and the Vega of an Option.

When you are buying options, it is important to notice the amount of Open Interest for the option that you are buying. Open Interest measures the amount of contracts that have already been traded for the particular option that you are trading. When the open interest is low, the spread between the bid and the ask price will be wide, making it much more difficult to make money on an option (BTO and STC) trade.

The open interest should be 1,000 contracts or more and we will only trade a maximum of 10% of the open interest.

This is important in that to have a successful option buying trade, you will have to sell the option before it expires to make a profit. If the open interest is low, it may be hard to sell the option at a favourable price.

Open Interest is a very useful tool to predict what price a share may trade at on the close of an options expiration day. If the maximum amount (and a significant amount) of open interest is beside a certain strike price in the option display window, there is a very strong possibility that, on the expiration day, the share price will close above that strike price if puts or below the strike price if calls (depending upon if it is a call or a put option).

The correct terminology for buying an option is Buy to Open (BTO).

The correct terminology to sell an option that you bought is Sell to Close (STC).

When you buy options, it is very possible that the trade will go against you sometimes. Therefore, it is important to protect all option purchases with OCO trades to minimise the losses to no more than 20% and maximise the gains.

It is not enough to simply buy an option and hope that it increases in value. Many people trade the stock market on a drug called 'Hopium'; hope is not a smart investment strategy!

For tax purposes, it is important to know that you can only claim a loss on options trade if you close the position. If you allow an option trade that has gone against you to expiry without closing the trade, you will not be able to claim that trade as a loss for tax accounting purposes.

Actions to take to buy and sell options

When buying and selling options
Online, the correct actions are
Buy to Open and *Sell to Close*

For taxation purposes and to be able to claim losses
against gains, always sell to close
options rather than let them expire with no value

Rho

Rho relates to the value of options at different interest rates. All you need to know for now is that during times of high interest rates, option premiums are higher, which is good news if you primary purpose is to sell options. Also, during uncertain times in the Stock Market when the CBOE VIX levels are high, premiums are also high. Strangely enough, we make more money from selling call and put option premiums during times of uncertainty and high interest rates because we know how to turn this to our advantage and you will to after reading and applying the knowledge in this book.

5 Rules for Option Buying Selection

1. Only invest 1/3 of your collected income from selling options

2. Buy Options with 60 to 90 days to go to expiration

3. Buy options ITM with a delta close to 70

4. Open Interest of 1,000 or more and only trade 10% of the Open Interest

5. Set targets using OCO trades to minimise loss to 20% (6% of the total) and maximise gains

Rules for option selection

1. Only invest 1/3 of your collected income from selling options

2. Buy options with 90 days to expiration

3. Buy options ITM with a delta close to 70

4. Open Interest of 1,000 or more and only trade 10% of the Open Interest

5. Set targets using OCO trades to minimise loss to 20% (6% of the total) and maximise gains

Chapter 2

Selling call options

The best time to sell call options is at the top turning (resistance) points.

It is important to observe the price graph for the shares you own and count the number of times that the share rolls between a low point and a high point in a specific trend.

The majority of the times, after a share price rolls three times in a specific direction, the share price will change direction.

The best time to sell the call option is at the very top of the third roll.

The best time to sell a call option is when the share price is at resistance due to the following reasons:

1) If the share has arrived at a resistance high point, it is inevitable that the share price will then turn around and return back to a lower support price.

2) If the share price drops in value, your account value will drop in value as well.

3) You can be pro-active by selling a call option to capture the reduction in your account value before it happens.

4) You can collect the fall in your account value before it happens by selling an ITM call option with a lower strike price than the current price.

5) You can pick a strike price close to the anticipated future support price. In fact, if there is an abundance of the ITM time value in the call option, you will collect more than the fall before it happens: you collect the intrinsic value plus time value.

When you sell call options, it is important to study the option display and choose the strike price that will pay the most amount of time value.

The next step is to divide your call option income by the number of days before the expiration to calculate the amount of cents per share per day.

The most profitable approach is to pick the strike price and month that make the most 'cents' per day.

As we can see in the graph below, the highest time value premium is available close to the ATM strike prices.

Vega - Time Value Volatility

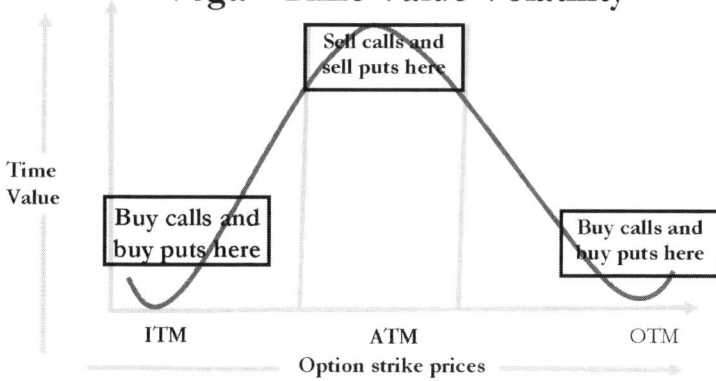

Time Value

Sell calls and sell puts here

Buy calls and buy puts here

Buy calls and buy puts here

ITM   ATM   OTM

Option strike prices

The best time to sell calls and buy puts is at the top of the 3rd Roll

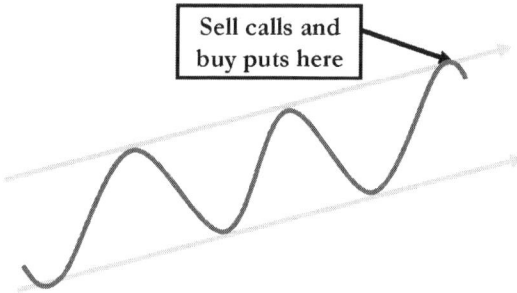

Sell calls and buy puts here

Chapter 3

Buy Put Options to profit from the downside

Now that you have collected the call option premium, as outlined in Chapter 2, it is time to learn how to buy put options to profit from the anticipated drop in share price.

As share prices drop in value, put options increase in value.

Put options will increase in value while the

share price decreases in value.

As options are highly risky to buy, make sure you follow the rules as below:

At resistance and top of 3rd roll, sell calls and use 1/3 of call income to buy puts

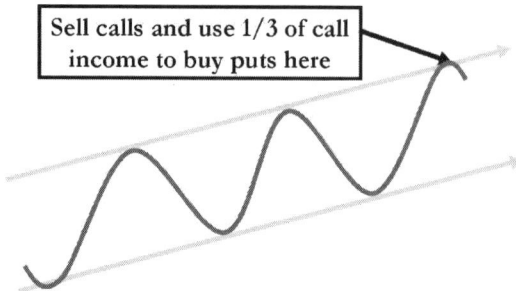

Sell calls and use 1/3 of call income to buy puts here

For example, collect $900 of call income and reinvest $300 to buy puts

Collect $900 of call income and reinvest $300 to buy puts here

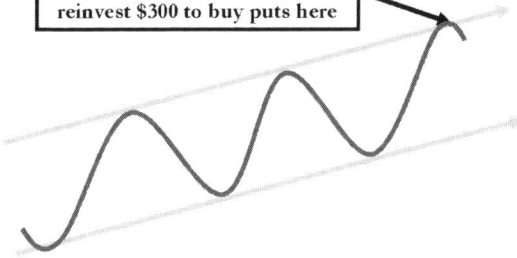

Rules for option selection

1. Only invest 1/3 of your collected income from selling options

2. Buy options with 90 days to expiration

3. Buy options ITM with a delta close to 70

4. Open Interest of 1,000 or more and only trade 10% of the Open Interest

5. Set targets using OCO trades to minimise loss to 20% (6% of the total) and maximise gains

When you have already collected the call option rent, you could reinvest one third of your income to buy a put option to profit from the downside.

The challenge for you now is: what is the best put option to buy?

For example, let us assume you have already collected $900 of call option income. One third of that is $300 ($900 / 3 = $300).

As we explained in Chapter 1, in order to capture the sweet spot, the best delta range is from 65 to 75.

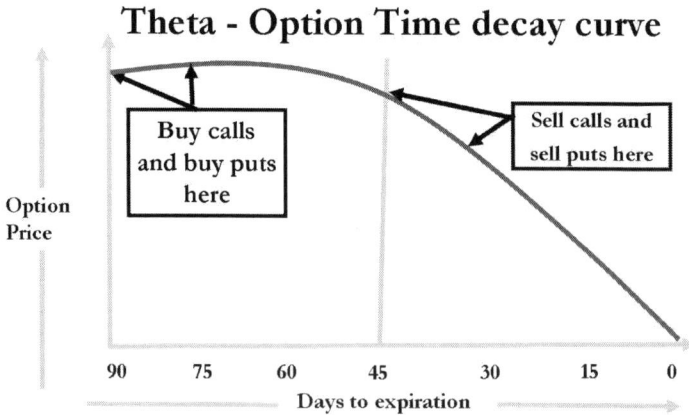

Theta - Option Time decay curve

Option Price

Buy calls and buy puts here

Sell calls and sell puts here

90   75   60   45   30   15   0

Days to expiration

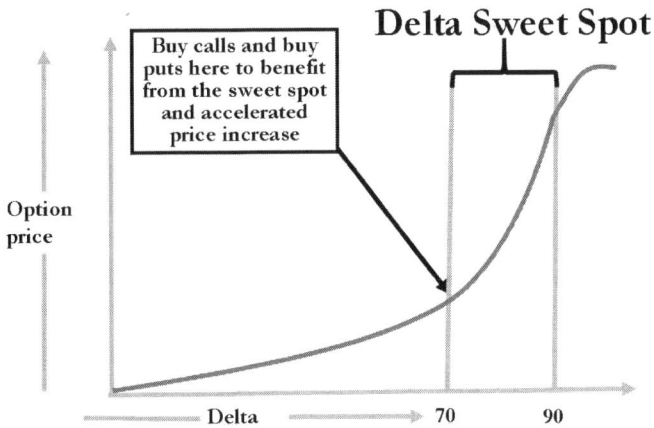

Delta Sweet Spot

Buy calls and buy puts here to benefit from the sweet spot and accelerated price increase

Option price

Delta 70 90

When you buy a put option, you will want to sell it as soon as possible, especially before it expires. To make sure you can sell it quickly, there needs to be an option open interest of at least 1,000. Make sure you buy no more than 10% of the open interest.

Delta is a very handy tool to predict the price of an option in the future.

Delta measures the relationship between the share price movement and the option price movement. In this regard, one can find out if the share price rises by $1 by how much will the option price increase by.

In the Option Display, the Delta is known as the Hedge Ratio (Hedge = h and Ratio = R) and so is displayed as c_hr or p_hr in the Option Display (c = call and p = put options).

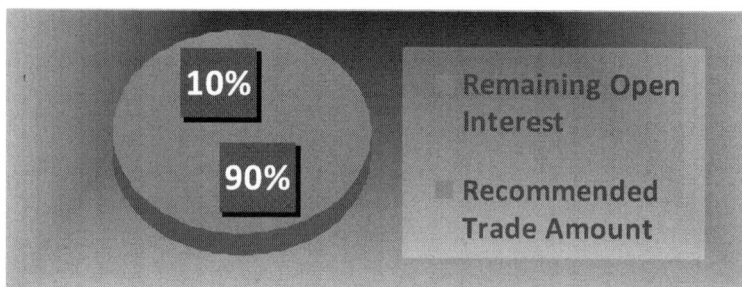

Always buy more time than you think you need, since many times you may have chosen the right put option strike price but the wrong month. In the past, our members have picked the correct strike price but not the correct month, thus the trade that they prepared did exactly as expected but they ran out of time to profit from the trade.

That is why it is very important that you always allow one month more than you think you need.

Remember that in order for an option purchase trade to be successful, you must buy and sell the option (close positions) before the option expires. All options have a finite life span; therefore, if you do not take your profit off the table before the option expiry date, you will lose all your profit.

When you buy a put option, you run the risk of losing all of your investment. After you have bought the put option, you can place an automatic trade that will both minimise loss and maximise gain. This is called an OCO (Order Cancels Order) trade. This OCO trade allows you to predetermine your exit points from the trade. The goal is to only lose 20% of the 1/3 (6% loss of profits at maximum) or make up to 100%. The OCO trade allows you to protect your profit and stay in the trade for more gains if you adjust the targets once the share price has started to move in the direction that you anticipated.

As you can see from the graph below, if you buy an option with 90 days before expiration date, it will hold its value for the first 45 days. Then, it starts declining rapidly in the last 45 days. This is why many investors lose money buying options, as they do not understand that time decay (theta) is more relevant than delta during the last 45 days before the expiration date. For example, in only one day, your option position may gain 10 cents of delta growth while, at the same time, lose 10 cents of time value.

Once an option trade starts to go against you, you are better off to close the trade early and only lose 20% of your initial investment.

To summarise the process:

1. You buy your share at support

2. You sell your call option at resistance

3. You buy your put option at resistance with 1/3 of your call option income

4. You place an OCO trade to protect profit and maximise gain

5. One of the OCO trades gets triggered and the trade is completed

If you follow the 5 steps as above, you will keep at least 90% of the rent you collected when you sold the call option in step 2 above.

3 Steps to Trade at the bottom of 3rd roll

1) Sell Maximum Time Value Put Option (+$900)
2) Use 1/3 of Put income to buy call Option (-$300)
3) Use OCO order to minimise loss / maximise gain

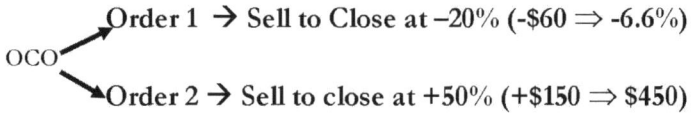

OCO

Order 1 → Sell to Close at −20% (-$60 ⟹ -6.6%)

Order 2 → Sell to close at +50% (+$150 ⟹ $450)

Chapter 4

How to place the trades on line

1. You buy your share at support

2. You sell your call option at resistance

3. You buy your put option at resistance with 1/3 of your call option income

4. You place an OCO trade to protect profit and maximise gain

5. One of the OCO trades gets triggered and the trade is completed

Step 1 – Buy shares at support

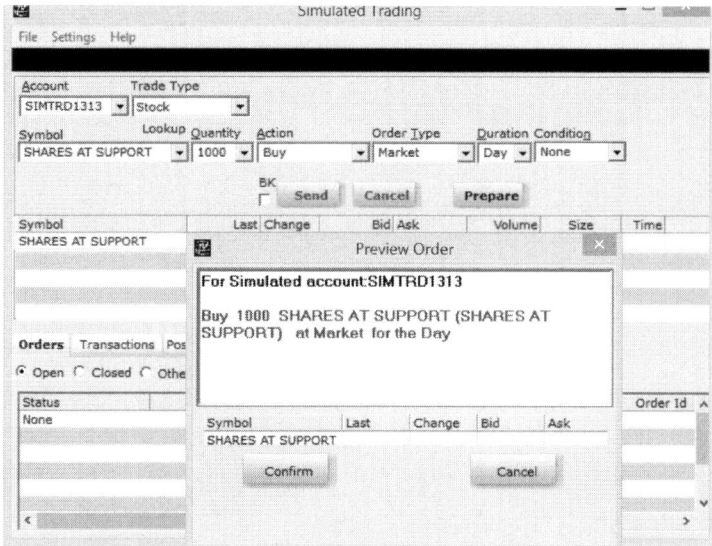

Step 2 – Sell Call Option at resistance, i.e., at the top of a roll

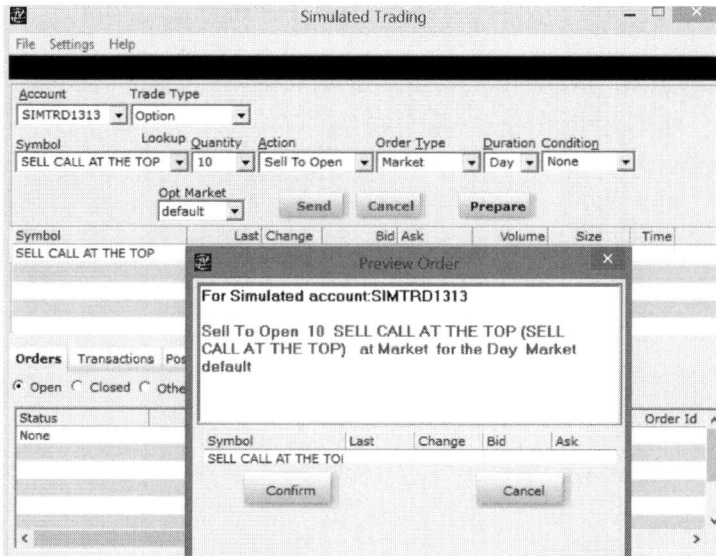

Step 3 – Buy put option at the top of the roll investing 1/3 of the call option income

To calculate the budget to spend on the put option, take your total income from selling the call option and divide it by three. Then, take that figure and divide it by the price of the put option that you plan to buy. Then, take that figure and divide by 100 to calculate the number of contracts that you can buy to stay close to the budget of 1/3.

For example, if you sell 10 contracts of a call option for $0.90 per share, you receive a total of $900. You divide this figure by 3 to calculate that your budget to buy put options, which results in $300. Then, take the $300 and divide it by the price of the put option that you are buying using the five rules.

If your put option is priced at $1, $300 divided by $1 = 300 shares, which, divided by 100 give us the number of contracts. In this case, 3 contracts.

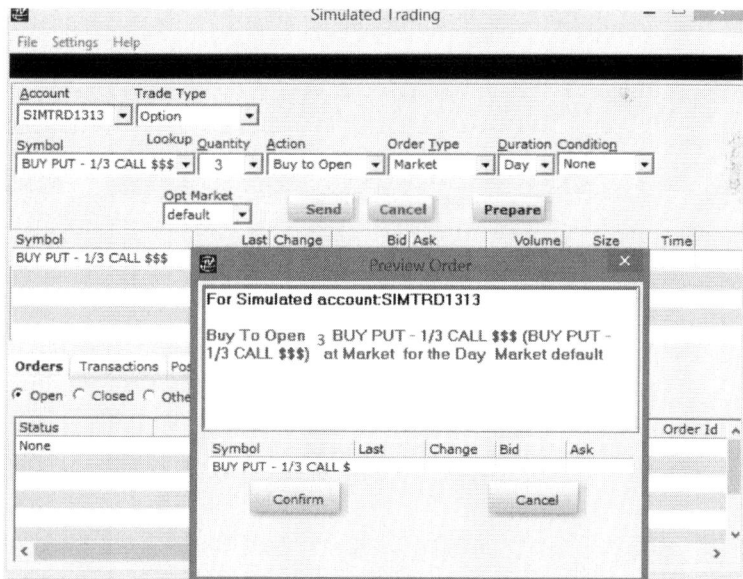

Step 4 – Place an OCO order to both protect (-20%) and profit (+100%) at the same time

Step 5 – one of the trades automatically gets triggered

Chapter 5

Sell Put Options at the bottom of support prices

Selling Put options

The best time to sell put options is at the bottom turning (support) points.

It is important to observe the price graph for the shares you own and count the number of times that the share rolls between a low point and a high point in a specific trend.

The majority of the times, after a share price rolls three times in a specific direction, the share price will change direction.

The best time to sell the put option is at the bottom of the third roll.

The best time to sell a put option is when the share price is both at support and at the bottom of third roll down of a downtrend. It is at this point that there is maximum possibility of the share price rising significantly after you have placed the put selling trade.

If the share has arrived at a support low point, it is inevitable that the share price will then turn around and return back to a high resistance price. Selling puts at support is a powerful strategy for making money when shares move from support to resistance.

Once your account value reaches $25,000 (cash plus shares or all shares), you can apply to your broker to get permission to sell naked put options.

Once you have sold a put option, there are four possible outcomes:

1. On the expiration day, share price closes above the strike price that we sold. In this case, there is no further action required and we keep all the option premium collected.

2. On the expiration day, share price closes below the strike price that we sold and accept the shares.

3. It looks like, on the expiration day, the share price will close below the strike price. We always have the possibility to buy back the put option for profit/loss to avoid the shares being put to us. You would buy back the put option for profit when the share has reached its resistance point. This would release the buying power to go and place another put selling trade in another company that you can find at support.

4. It looks like, on the expiration day, the share price will close below the strike price. We always have the possibility to buy back the put option for profit/loss and sell the next month at the same or a different strike price. When doing this trade, one should aim to create a credit trade. Credit trade means the income from the next month put option sold is greater than the cost to buy back the put option for the current month.

When calculating the profit for a put selling trade, one should consider the Return On Capital Employed (ROCE). As one is not investing money to sell a put option, the calculation is not a Return On Investment (ROI).

When you sell put options, it is important to study the option display and choose the strike price that will pay the most amount of time value.

The next step is to divide your put option income by the number of days before the expiration. This way, we calculate the amount of cents per share per day.

The most profitable approach is to pick the strike price and month that make the most 'cents'.

As we can see in the graph below, the highest time value premium is available close to the ATM strike prices.

Vega - Time Value Volatility

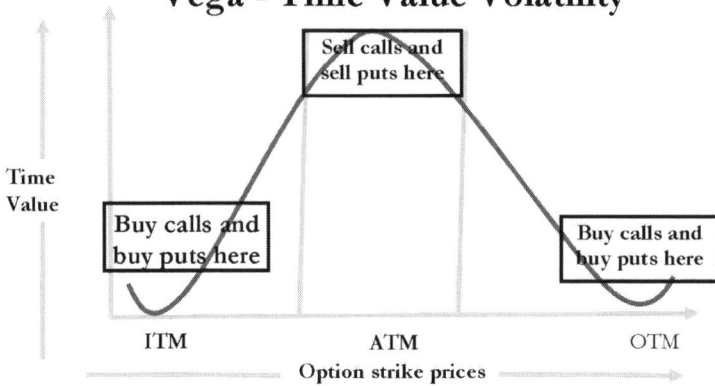

Time Value (vertical axis)

Sell calls and sell puts here

Buy calls and buy puts here

Buy calls and buy puts here

ITM   ATM   OTM

Option strike prices

One should only sell puts on shares that have been carefully researched using the TICN 4 step system as explained in the book *So... you want to be Financially Free?*, http://www.tinyurl.com/previewticnbook

When selling a put option at support, we could choose one of 4 strike prices:

1. A strike price lower than support. We call this a 'conservative approach'. In this case, it is very unlikely that the shares will be put to us; therefore, no further action may be required (NAR).

2. A strike price at support. We call this a 'neutral approach'. In this case, it is not likely that the shares will be put to us; therefore, no further action may be required (NAR).

3. A strike price higher than support. We call this an 'aggressive approach'. In this case, the shares may well be put to us; therefore, some action may be required to decide whether we want to accept the shares or push the put option price forward to another month to help postpone the decision to accept the shares or not (AR).

4. A strike price two strikes higher than support. We call this a 'super aggressive approach'. In this case, it is very likely that the shares will be put to us; therefore, some action may be required to decide whether we want to accept the shares or push the put option price forward to another month to help postpone the decision to accept the shares or not (AR).

The 3 x 3 selling put strategy

When selling put options, the most profitable approach (8%) has proved to be a combination of ATM, OTM and ITM put options. In order to achieve this, we build a 3 x 3 matrix as follows:

$27,000	Co. 1 $9,000	Co. 2 $9,000	Co. 3 $9,000	
Strike C	NA	AR	AR	Aggressive: 6%
Strike B	NA	NA	AR	Neutral: 4%
Strike A	NA	NA	NA	Conservative: 2%
A<B<C	Goes up	*Slightly above strike price*	Goes down	*Average: 4%*

Where:

1. We allocate a $27,000 budget for this strategy

2. 1/3 Company A: we allocate $9,000 to Company A

3. 1/3 Company B: we allocate $9,000 to Company B

4. 1/3 Company C: we allocate $9,000 to Company C

5. 1/3 OTM: we allocate $3,000 to selling OTM conservative put options

6. 1/3 ATM we allocate $3,000 to selling ATM neutral put options

7. 1/3 ITM we allocate $3,000 to selling ITM aggressive put options

On average, with ~ 30 days to option expiration date:

OTM put option sales yield 2% ROCE
ATM put option sales yield 4% ROCE
ITM put option sales yield 6% ROCE

We call this a 'blended approach' to put selling and the average of all three can yield 4%.

If one uses the extra buying power available in their account, then this potential 4% can be further leveraged up to as high as 8%.

When one applies this blended approach across three companies (1/3 ITM: 1/3 OTM: 1/3 ATM), 9 put selling trades are placed. On average, on the expiration day, 6 out of the 9 positions can end up above their respective strike prices with no further action required (NAR) Conversely, on average 3 out of the 9 positions can end up below their respect strike prices and some further action may be required (AR).

The above assumption is based upon if you trade 3 companies at support and, on the expiration day:

-   One share price rises two strike prices and closes above all 3 strike prices

-   One share price stays at the same level and remains above two strike prices

-   One share price drops one strike price and remains below two strike prices

In summary, it may be hard to believe that one can make money from selling put options without having to invest any money. However, for those of you that may have a challenge with the concept of making money without having to invest, remember that you are still adding some value by selling puts: you are adding value to someone on the other side of your put selling trade, as they may have wanted to buy a put option to protect their investment in their shares. Therefore, you are adding value by providing 'peace of mind' to the buyer, a priceless human emotion brought in by the fact that you are creating an environment where their investments are protected. You can also say you are contributing to their SWAN factor! (Sleep Well at Night).

Once you have reached a value of $25,000 in your account, you have permission to sell put options. This is a very powerful way to leverage the extra buying power in your account.

When you sell an option for shares to be possibly put to you in the future, there are four possible outcomes to this put selling trade:

1) On the expiration date of the put option that you sold, the share price closes above the strike price of this put option that you sold. In this case, the shares will not be put to you and no further action is required. NAR = No Action Required.

2) On the expiration date of the put option that you sold, the share price closes below the strike price of this put option that you sold. In this case, the shares will be put to you; if you are still happy to own those shares, no further action is required.

However, if you are only in the business of selling put options to accumulate income and do not want shares put to you then you can take the following action: AR = Action Required:

3) Before the expiration date of the put option that you sold, you can always buy back the put option to avoid the possibility of the shares being put to you.

Once you have sold a put option, and if the share price begins to rise, the put option that you sold will rapidly lose value in your favour. If for example, you sold a put option and received $1 with 6 weeks to go to the expiration date and if after one week it is now only worth $0.20, you have already enjoyed 80% of the benefit of the trade if you close the trade and buy back the put option for $0.20. This action will free up your buying power to move onto another put selling opportunity in the market.

This is in line with the Law of Diminishing Returns in that there is no point trying to make those last $0.20 with 5 weeks to go when there may be other possibilities to make way more than $0.20 in other put selling trades during those 5 weeks.

Before the expiration date of the put option that you sold, you can always buy back the put option to avoid the possibility of the shares being put to you and roll the trade forward to the next month or subsequent months to delay/postpone the possibility of the shares being put to you. When you push forward a put selling trade out to a future month, you will receive a credit into your account as the income from selling a future month is greater than the cost of buying back the current month put option. You create a net credit into your account which can be added to the initial credit that you received when you sold the first put.

Chapter 6

Buy Call Options to profit from the upside

Now that you have collected the put option premium, as outlined in Chapter 5, it is time to learn how to buy call options to profit from the anticipated rise in share price.

As share prices rise in value, call options will increase in value.

As it is highly dangerous to buy options, make sure you follow the rules as below:

Rules for option selection

1. Only invest 1/3 of your collected income from selling options

2. Buy options with 90 days to expiration

3. Buy options ITM with a delta close to 70

4. Open Interest of 1,000 or more and only trade 10% of the Open Interest

5. Set targets using OCO trades to minimise loss to 20% (6% of the total) and maximise gains

When you have already collected the put option rent, you could reinvest one third of your income to buy a call option to profit from the upside.

The challenge for you now is: what is the best call option to buy?

For example, let us assume you have already collected $900 of put option income. One third of that is $300 ($900 / 3 = $300).

As we explained in Chapter 1, in order to capture the sweet spot, the best delta range is from 65 to 75.

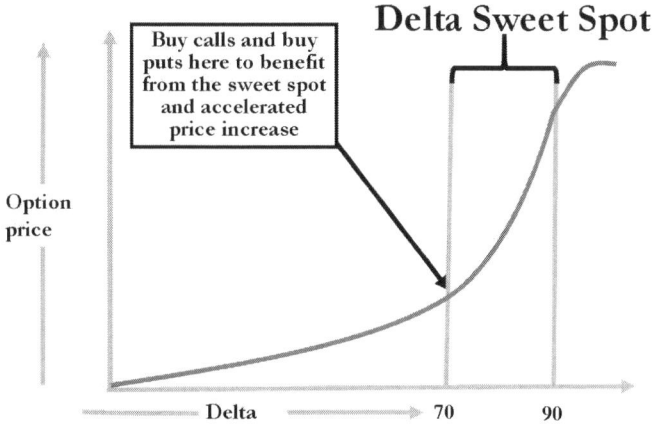

Delta Sweet Spot

Buy calls and buy puts here to benefit from the sweet spot and accelerated price increase

Option price

Delta   70   90

When you buy a call option, you will want to sell it as soon as possible, especially before it expires. To make sure you can sell it quickly, there needs to be an option open interest of at least 1,000. Make sure you buy no more than 10% of the open interest.

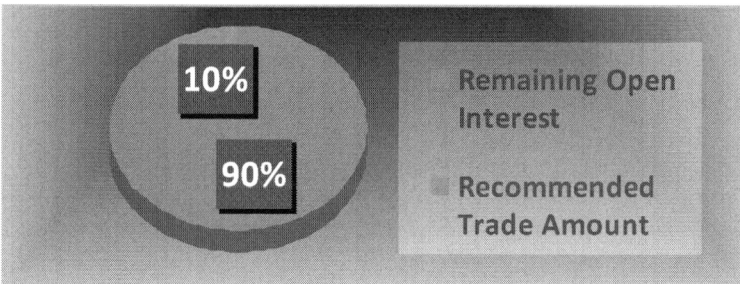

10%   Remaining Open Interest

90%   Recommended Trade Amount

Always buy more time than you think you need, since many times you may have chosen the right call option strike price but the wrong month. In the past, our members have picked the correct strike price but not the correct month, thus the trade that they prepared did exactly as expected but they ran out of time to be able to profit from the trade. That is why it is very important that you always allow one month more than you think you need.

Remember that, in order for an option purchase trade to be successful, you must buy and sell the option (close positions) before the option expires. All options have a finite life span; therefore, if you do not take your profit off the table before the option expiry date, you will lose all your profit.

When you buy a call option, you run the risk of losing all of your investment. That is why, right after you have bought the call option, you can place an automatic trade that will both minimise loss and maximise gain.

This is called an OCO (Order Cancels Order) trade. This OCO trade allows you to predetermine your exit points from the trade. The goal is to only lose 20% (6% of the initial amount) or make up to 100%. The OCO trade allows you to protect your profit and stay in the trade for more gains if you adjust the targets once the share price has started to move in the direction that you anticipated.

As you can see from the graph below, if you buy an option with 90 days before expiration date, it will hold its value for the first 45 days. Then, it starts declining rapidly in the last 45 days. This is why many investors lose money buying options, as they do not understand that time decay (theta) is more relevant than delta during the last 45 days before the expiration date. For example, in only one day, your option position may gain 10 cents of delta growth while, at the same time, lose 10 cents of time value.

Once an option trade starts to go against you, you are better off to close the trade early and only lose 20% of your investment.

To summarise the process:

1. You sell a put at support

2. You buy a call option at support

3. You buy the call option at support using 1/3 of your put option income

4. You place an OCO trade to protect profit and maximise gain

5. One of the OCO trades gets triggered and the trade is completed

If you follow the 5 steps as above, you will keep at least 90% of the rent you collected when you sold the call option in step 2 above.

At support and bottom of 3rd roll, sell puts and buy calls with 1/3 of the put income

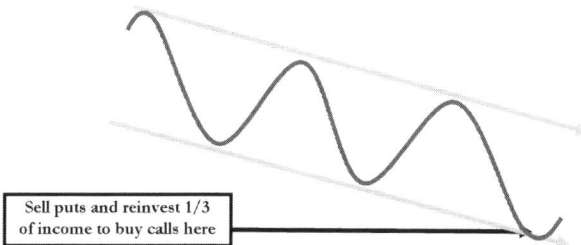

Sell puts and reinvest 1/3 of income to buy calls here

For example, collect $900 of put income and reinvest $300 to buy calls

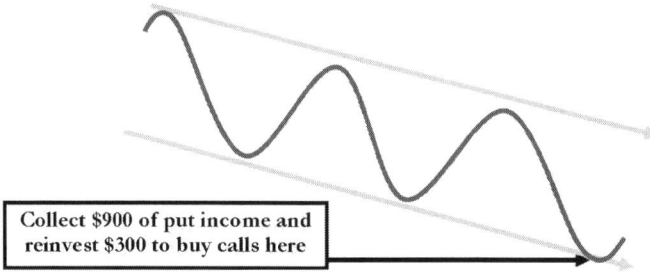

Collect $900 of put income and reinvest $300 to buy calls here

3 Steps to Trade at the bottom of 3rd roll

1) Sell Maximum Time Value Put Option (+$900)
2) Use 1/3 of Put income to buy call Option (-$300)
3) Use OCO order to minimise loss / maximise gain

OCO
- Order 1 → Sell to Close at –20% (-$60 ⇒ -6.6%)
- Order 2 → Sell to close at +50% (+$150 ⇒ $450)

Chapter 7

How to place trades on line

To summarise the process:

1. You sell a put at support

2. You buy a call option at support

3. You buy the call option at support using 1/3 of your put option income

4. You place an OCO trade to protect profit and maximise gain

5. One of the OCO trades gets triggered and the trade is completed

Step 1 – Sell a put Option at support

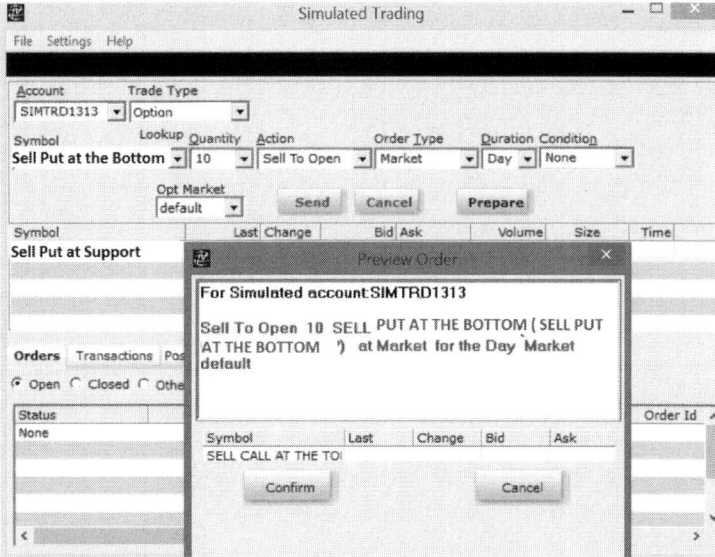

Step 2 – Buy a Call Option at Support

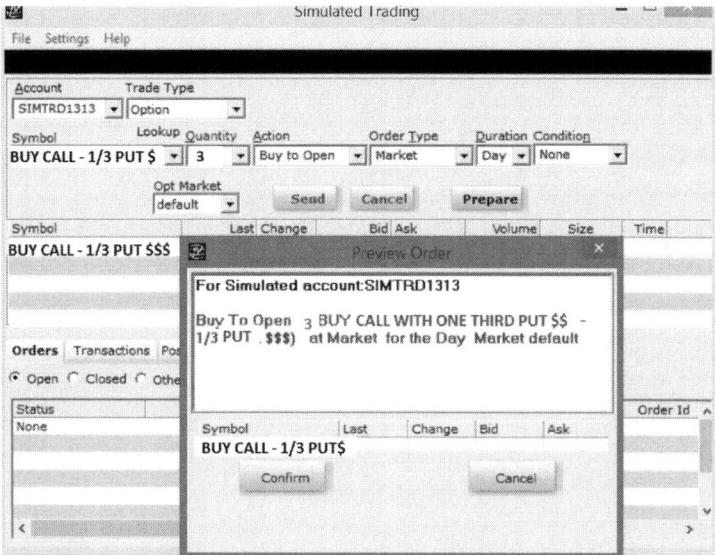

Step 3 – Buy a call option with 1/3 of the income from selling the put option

To calculate the budget to spend on the call option, take your total income from selling the put option and divide it by three. Then, take that figure and divide it by the price of the call option that you plan to buy. Take that figure and divide it by 100 in order to calculate the number of contracts that you can buy to stay close to the budget of 1/3.

For example, if you sell 10 contracts of a put option for $0.90 per share to receive a total of $900, dividing this figure by 3 gives us a budget to buy call options of $300. By dividing this $300 by the price of the call option, we calculate how many contracts to buy using the five rules.

In this regard, if your call option is priced at $1, $300 divided by $1 = 300 shares, i.e., 3 contracts.

Step 4 – Place an OCO order to protect profit and maximise potential gains

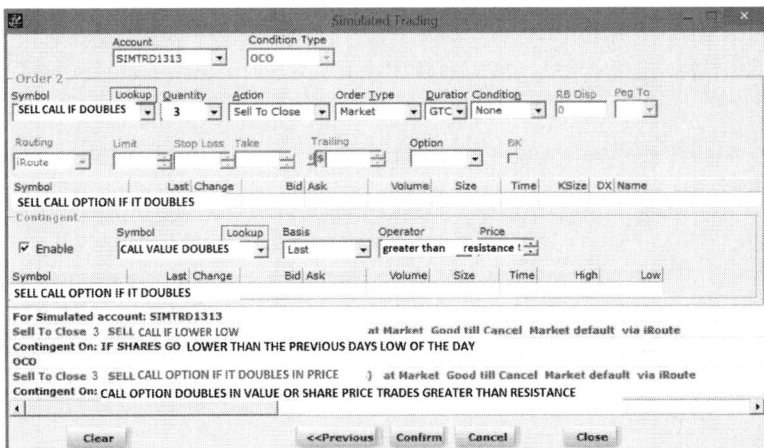

Step 5 - One of the OCO trades gets triggered and the trade is completed

Chapter 8

Case studies selling puts

In the example as below, a put option was sold at the wrong time, in that share was clearly at resistance having already grown by 200% from $6 to $18 previous to this trade.

This is great example of how you can use time value and volatility to trade your way out of trouble on a loss making trade and turn a poor trade into a profitable trade.

On the 25th January 2013, 10 contracts of the FEB $18 put were sold for $1.74 per share, yielding a total income of $1,744.56. At this point, the share was at a price of ~ $18 and, at a resistance point, both from a price performance perspective and reading the chart indicators as below:

Price graph for BBRY 25ᵗʰ Jan 2013

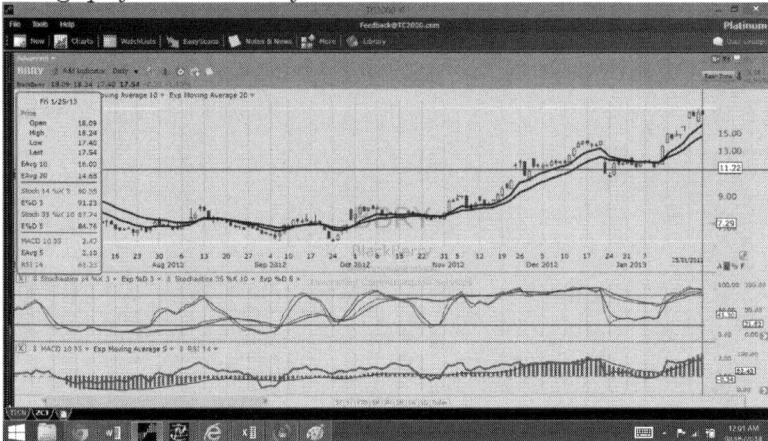

On 6ᵗʰ February 2013, when the share price was trading at $15 and to avoid the shares being put to the account at the agreed price of $18 resulting in a drop in account value of $3, the FEB $18 put option was bought back for $2.34 per share, that is, a total cost of $2,335.38. At the same time and date, on the 6ᵗʰ of February, the MAR $15 put option was sold for $1.19 per share, yielding an income of $1.194.57. This action turned the trade back into a profitable trade of $603.75 ($1,744.56 - $2,335.38 + $1,194 = $603.75, provide the share price could close above $15 on the 3ʳᵈ Friday expiration date of March 2013).

Price graph for BBRY 6th February

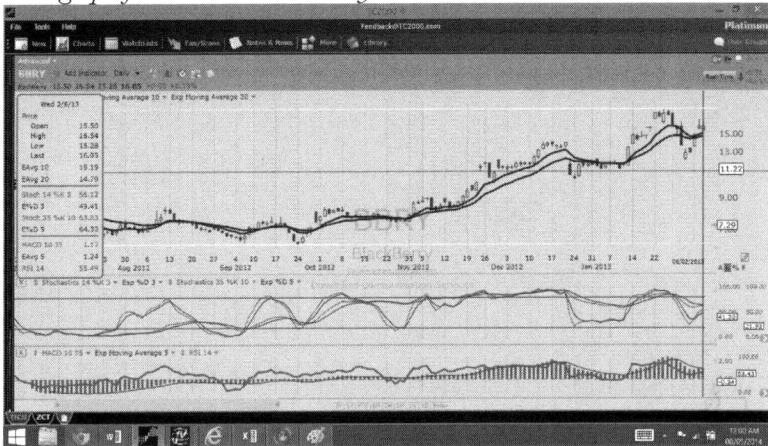

However, the share price continued to fall, so on the 15th March (again, to avoid the shares being put to the account at the agreed strike price of $15), when the shares were now trading at $15.20, thus risking a share value loss of $0.20, the MAR $15 put option was bought back for $0.24, total cost of $235.38.

Price graph for BBRY 15th March

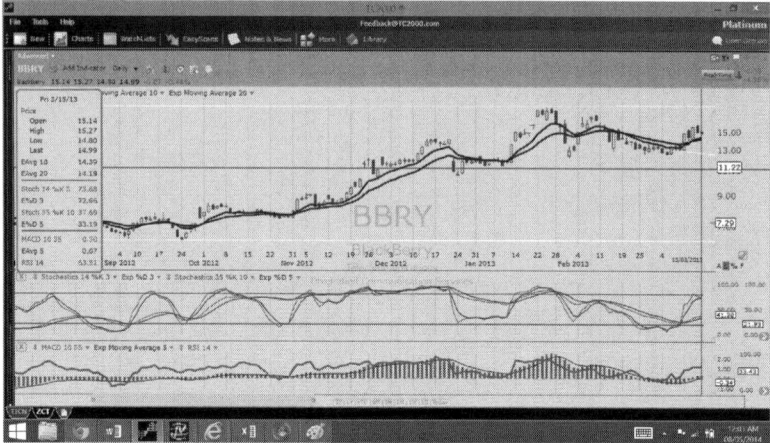

At the same date and time, the APR $11 put was sold for $254.59, which produced a final profit of $622.96, provided the share price ended up above $11 on the third Friday of April.

As we can see from the graph as below, the share price did indeed end up above $11 on the 3rd Friday expiration date of April. Therefore, what could have been a $6,000 loss of an account value was converted into a total profit of $622.96 and a ROCE of 3.35%.

Price graph for BBRY on 3rd Friday 19th April

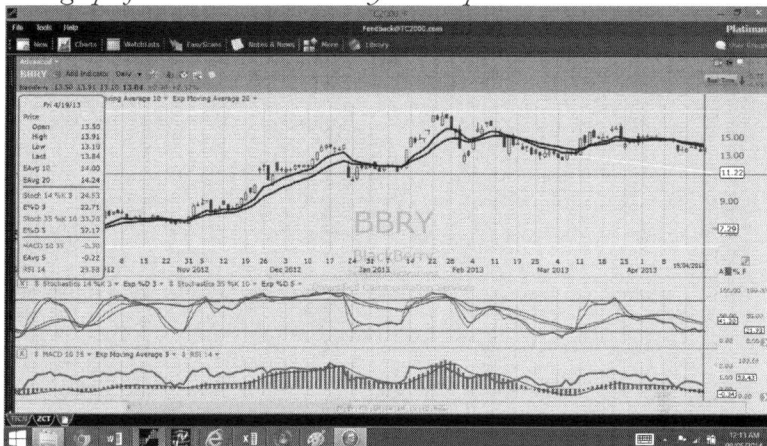

The lesson to be learned from this trade is, first of all, <u>do not sell puts at extreme highs</u> when the indicators are showing you potential for the share price to fall.

However, if a put trade goes against you as this one did, it is important not to panic and use your new found knowledge of time value to trade your way out of a poor trade to turn it into a profitable trade.

Once a week, we hold a webinar called 'Bottom Fishing'. This webinar helps you find suitable put selling opportunities in the market. This webinar can be booked via www.ticn.com.

Find below a summary table of the trades referred to in the example above:

Trade date	Trade action	Company name	Number, amount	Price, $	Put Option income
25/01/13	Sell to Open	BBRY Feb13 18P	10	1.74	1,744.56
06/02/13	Buy to Close	BBRY Feb13 18P	10	2.34	(-2,335.38)
06/02/13	Sell to Open	BBRY Mar13 15P	10	1.19	1,194.57
15/03/13	Buy to Close	BBRY Mar13 15P	10	0.24	(-235.38)
15/03/13	Sell to Open	BBRY Apr13 11P	10	0.25	254.59
Final profit					622.96

Chapter 9

Bonus strategy if you do not have $25,000 to trade with

It is said that 95% of people do not read a book beyond the third chapter. Therefore, we want to congratulate you and reward you for reading this far with a powerful bonus strategy. This is for you or your club if you or your club does not yet have $25,000 to trade with.

You can only sell puts with an account that is valued at $25,000, so for accounts that are at $2,000 and that have had prior clearance from the broker to trade spreads, here is what you can do: you can pick a stock that is at an extreme support level like a strong 4 x 4 company that is at a 10 year extreme share price low point. You can then place the following trade:

Step 1: Buy to Open a put strike price 2 to 3 strike prices lower than the strike price you plan to sell.

Step 2: Sell to Open a put strike price just below the current support levels.

If, for example, you buy a $5 put and sell $7 put, you only require the buying power of $2 x the number contracts that you both buy and sell.

Your risk in the trade is $2 and your reward is the credit you receive for placing the trade.

Your reward could be as high as 30 cents per share. Since your risk is $2, your return on capital employed would be 15%.

Like any high reward strategy, there is a high risk and this is a gentle introduction to you into trading credit spreads or, as we say, *Zero Cost Trades*.

It is highly recommended that you would practice this high reward/high risk trade with your simulated account first.

If the share price in the example above ends up below the $7 strike price on the expiration date, you could lose $2 x the number of contracts traded minus your original credit.

Before the option expiration date, you do have the choice to push the strike prices forward to another month in the future to allow more time for the share price to close above $7.

Pushing forward may give you an additional credit as a benefit to you put will reduce your return per time as now your return is over a couple of months and not once month as previously anticipated when you placed the trade.

We do provide a once per week live seminar on this called *Zero Cost Trades* at 7 pm GMT on Monday evenings if you wish more help and guidance with this type of trade. It is also explained in much more detail in http://www.tinyurl.com/zerocosttrades

Chapter 10

Summary

In summary, it is important to understand options in more depth if we wish to earn more money from trading options.

It is said that, to catch a thief, you have to know a thief. Equally, to catch more income from options it is important to know more about options.

There are times when options are in what we call 'theft mode', that is, they are totally overpriced to buy but represent for you an opportunity to make a great returns to sell those overpriced options.

The best way to learn is to do and the best way to apply this knowledge that we have shared with you is to first practice with the simulator and then practice for real with a small number of contracts first.

The next level of knowledge available for you to help you gain greater returns is to read and apply the strategies taught to you in our next two books:

1. *Zero Cost Trades*, available to download on http://www.tinyurl.com/zerocosttrades

2. *Dare to Debit Spread*, also available to download on http://www.tinyurl.com/daretodebit

We look forward to you applying your new found knowledge from this book.

Please, let us know how this book has helped you understand options better. Also let us know about any of your successful options trades.

Always know why you are placing a trade, what profit you want from the option trade, what are your exit points and what are your protection levels for the trade.

Always use the markets money and not your money when it comes to buying options.

Your next step is to now visit us on www.ticn.com and start your evaluation, education and application process. Before you apply to join one of our clubs, you can observe how we make money during a live monthly club meeting.

To join a club, please, visit http://www.ticn.com/ and click on the relevant country in the world map.

If you have any questions and want to know how we can help and support you, you can reach us on owen@ticn.com or +353 74 91 59 763.

owen@ticn.com
www.ticn.com
Skype: ticnowen
www.linkedin.com/oweno
malley

Yours to serve,
Owen O'Malley
CEO of TICN Ltd.